PREPARATORY BOOK A

The ALL-IN-ONE

APPROACH to

Succeeding at the Piano®

 with CD

by HELEN MARLAIS

MOZART   HAYDN   BEETHOVEN

Name: _____

Teacher: _____

Beginning Date: _____

Let's Begin Piano Lessons!

ISBN-13: 978-1-61928-103-5

T H E
F·J·H
MUSIC
COMPANY
I N C.
Frank J. Hackinson

Production: Frank J. Hackinson
Production Coordinators: Peggy Gallagher and Philip Groeber
Editors: Edwin McLean and Peggy Gallagher
Art Direction: Andi Whitmer – in collaboration with Helen Marlais
Cover Illustration: © 2014 Susan Hellard /Arena
Interior Illustrations: © 2010 Susan Hellard /Arena & © 2014 Teresa Robertson/Arena
Cover and Interior Illustration Concepts: Helen Marlais
Engraving: Tempo Music Press, Inc.
Printer: Tempo Music Press, Inc.

TABLE OF CONTENTS

FJH2223

COMPOSERS AND ARRANGERS

Timothy Brown: Student solos: p. 42, 49
Lyrics: p. 30, 42, 49
Duet parts: p. 28, 42, 48, 49

Kevin Costley: Student solos: p. 40, 47
Lyrics: p. 40, 47
Duet part: p. 47

Mary Leaf: Student solos: p. 13, 14, 15, 17, 19, 22
Lyrics: p. 13, 14, 15, 17, 19, 22, 32
Duet parts: p. 13, 17, 19, 35

Helen Marlais: Student solos: p. 6, 10, 12, 21, 23, 24, 28, 32, 35, 39, 44, 45, 48
Lyrics: p. 8, 10, 21, 23, 24, 35, 39, 44, 45
Duet parts: p. 10, 23

Edwin McLean: Student solos: p. 8, 9, 25
Lyrics: p. 9, 12, 25
Duet parts: p. 22, 25, 31, 32

Kevin Olson: Student solos: p. 31, 36, 37
Lyrics: p. 31, 36, 37
Duet parts: p. 36, 37

Sitting at the Piano

1. ON THE BENCH

- With your hands in your lap, sit comfortably on the bench in the middle of the piano.

- Imagine a daisy growing through your spine and out the top of your head. Sit tall.

- Relax your shoulders and breathe easily.

- Use a stool under your feet if you can't reach the floor.

2. DISTANCE AND HEIGHT

- Place your hands over the white keys.

- The tip of your elbow should be at the same level as the TOP of the WHITE keys.

- Place a book on the bench to raise you up if you need it.

- Can you swing your arms gently from side to side? Notice your elbows will be slightly in **front** of your sides—not by your sides.

- Your forearms should be parallel with the floor.

FJH2223

3. PERFECT PIANO HANDS

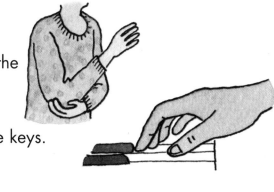

- Place your L.H. (left hand) on your right elbow. Notice the round shape. Notice the space between your fingers.

- Keeping the same shape, place your L.H. over the white keys. Then place your R.H. (right hand) on the white keys.

- Notice your 8 knuckles. They look like 8 small hills.

- Notice the letter "C" in your L.H. Then notice the letter "C" in your R.H. This is a natural hand position.

- Do your 5th fingers look like this? ⟶

- Close the fallboard. Tap your "Perfect Piano Hands" solidly 5 times.

4. FINGER NUMBERS

Every finger has a number.

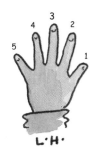
L·H·

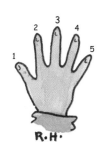
R·H·

Tap your fingertips together lightly 3 times:
- finger 1's together
- finger 2's together
- finger 3's together
- finger 4's together
- finger 5's together

With your R.H. wiggle:
- finger 1
- finger 4
- finger 5
- fingers 2 and 3 together

Now do the same with your L.H.

The Steady Beat

 All music has a beat.

1 1 1 1

With your teacher, Clap once for every note:

1. Count and clap aloud:

1 1 1 1

2. Walk around the room and swing your arms back and forth with every beat.

3. Sit on the piano bench and sway to the beat.

Teacher plays:

The Piano March

Note to Teachers: Play *The Piano March* for the student and have them do the 3 activities above.

FJH2223

The Keyboard

- The keys on the piano are white and black.

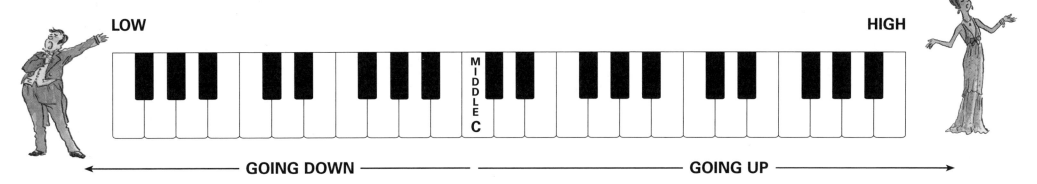

LOW   **HIGH**

MIDDLE C

◄──────── GOING DOWN ────────   ──────── GOING UP ────────►

Taking a Walk

L.H.

- Tap your L.H. fingers 1 and 2 lightly on your thigh 3 times.

- Notice the "C" shape between fingers 1 and 2.

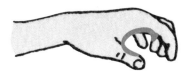

- Wiggle fingers 1 and 2.

- Start in the **middle** of the keyboard and play one key at a time, going **lower** (to the left.) Use fingers 1 and 2 together, at the same time.

R.H.

- Tap your R.H. fingers 1 and 2 lightly on your thigh 3 times.

- Notice the "C" shape between fingers 1 and 2.

- Wiggle fingers 1 and 2.

- Start in the **middle** of the keyboard and play one key at a time, going **higher** (to the right.) Do you see the "C" shape?

Note to Teachers: With eyes closed, can your student hear the difference between high and low? Up and down as you play several keys?

Groups of 2 Black Keys

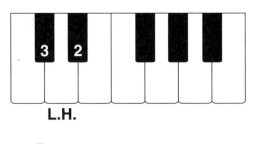

L.H.

To begin: 1. Raise your L.H. (left hand).
2. Wiggle fingers 2 and 3.
3. Gently push these fingers in your thigh.
4. Say the words in rhythm with your teacher.

CD 3, 4, 5 • MIDI 2

Hiking Up

Start in the LOW
part of the keyboard.

2

3   tain!

moun-

2

big

3

great

2

the

3

up

2

ing

3

Hik-

Now raise your R.H. Play the piece again using R.H. fingers 2 and 3.

Note to Teachers: Encourage students to play on their finger pads, without dents.
(A "dent" refers to a collapsed first knuckle joint.)
Have students drop into each note and keep a steady beat.

FJH2223

Groups of 3 Black Keys

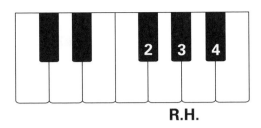

R.H.

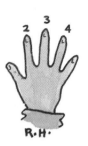

To begin: 1. Raise your R.H. (right hand).
2. Wiggle fingers 2, 3, and 4.
3. Gently push these fingers in your thigh.
4. Say the words in rhythm with your teacher.

Hiking Down

Start at the HIGH
part of the keyboard.

4
  3
Down   2
   we
    go,

4
  3
look 2
   be-
    low,

4
  3
we've 2
   had
    fun

4
  3
now 2
   we're
    done!

After you play the piece, raise your L.H. Play the piece again using L.H. fingers 2, 3, and 4.

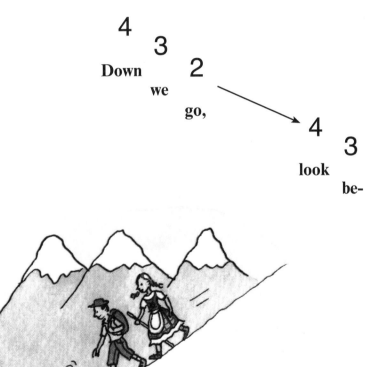

The Quarter Note ♩

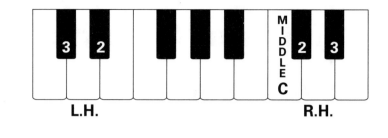

♩ This is a **quarter note**. It gets 1 beat.

Practice steps:

- Clap and step to this rhythm with a steady beat: ♩ ♩ ♩ ♩
  Each clap is 1 beat.

- Now tap *Keeping the Beat* on your lap,
  counting "1" aloud for each beat.

 CD 9, 10, 11 • MIDI 4

Keeping the Beat

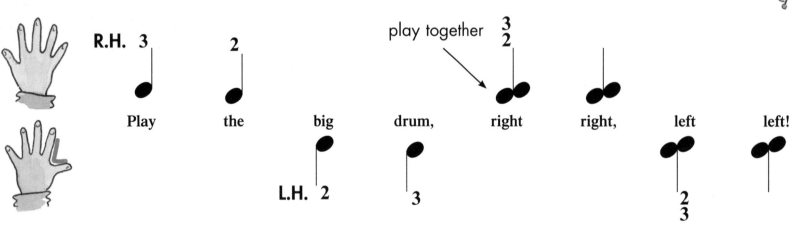

play together

R.H. 3   2   3/2

Play   the   big   drum,   right   right,   left   left!

L.H. 2   3   2/3

- Did you play with a steady beat?
- Did you make a big sound?

DUET PART: (student plays 1 octave lower)

mf

FJH2223

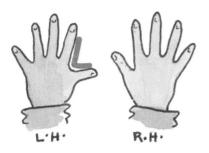

Note stem up = **R.H.**

Note stem down = **L.H.**

1. Draw note stems going **up** for the R.H.
The first one is done for you.

2. Draw note stems going **down** for the L.H.
The first one is done for you.

3. • Circle the notes for the R.H.
• Then tap and count, using the correct hands.
• Can you tap and say the words?

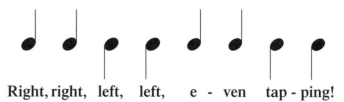

Right, right, left, left,   e - ven   tap - ping!

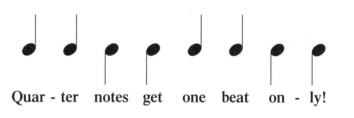

Quar - ter notes get one beat on - ly!

☐ Check the box
when you are done!

4. • Sit side by side with your teacher.
• Listen and watch your teacher tap a rhythm.
Then tap the same rhythm back.

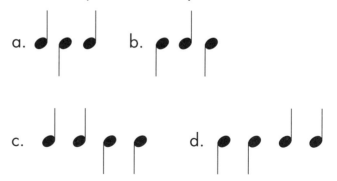

FJH2223

11

Practice steps:

- Notice the 2 groups of notes.
- Raise the hand that will start.
- Wiggle the fingers you will use.
- Gently press these fingers into your lap.
- Tap with your "Perfect Piano Hands" and count aloud.

Look! →

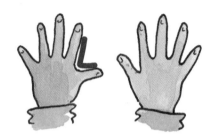

 CD 12, 13, 14 • MIDI 5

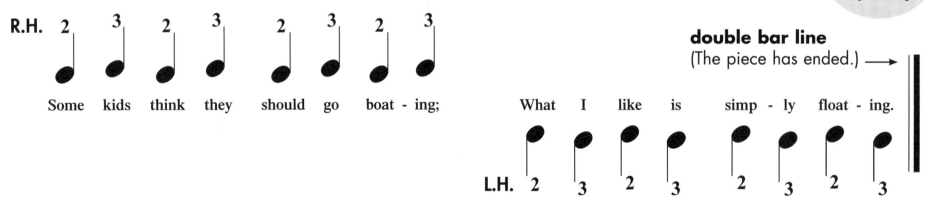

Happy Days

Lift your hands off the keys, wrists *first*, and place them in your lap.

R.H. 2 3 2 3 2 3 2 3

Some kids think they should go boat - ing;

double bar line
(The piece has ended.) →

What I like is simp - ly float - ing.

L.H. 2 3 2 3 2 3 2 3

FJH2223

Practice steps:

- Tell your teacher which group of notes go up, and which go down.

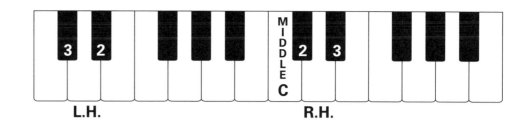

Yapping Puppy

R.H.   2   3   2   3   3   2   3   2

Lit - tle   pup - py,   quit   your   yap - ping!   Don't   you   think   you   should   be   nap - ping?

L.H.   3   2   3   2   2   3   2   3

DUET PART: (student plays 1 octave higher)

Practice steps:

- Tap the rhythm on the closed lid of the fallboard.
- Tap with your "Perfect Piano Hands."
- Count aloud "1" for each ♩.
- Tap and say the finger numbers.
- Tap and say the words.

Use these practice steps for every piece, every day!

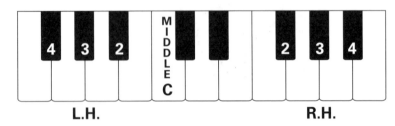

L.H.   R.H.

Little Cottontails

CD 18, 19, 20 • MIDI 7

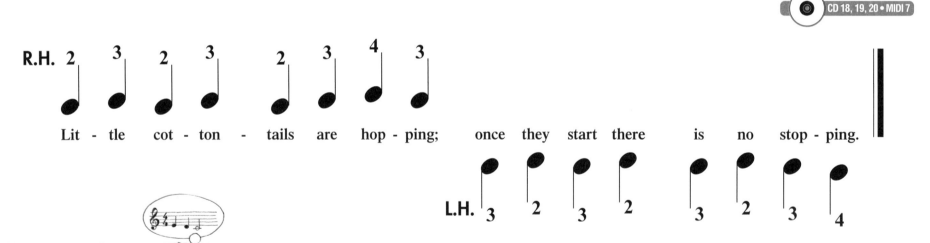

R.H. 2 3 2 3 2 3 4 3

Lit - tle   cot - ton - tails   are   hop - ping;   once   they   start   there   is   no   stop - ping.

L.H. 3 2 3 2 3 2 3 4

Time to Compose:

- Make up your own piece on the black keys about rabbits.

- Did you hear a steady beat?

Note to Teachers: Have students play each note with their forearm and wrist parallel, moving as one unit. Have students do this for every piece in the book for excellent technique.

Practice steps:

- Each ♩ gets ____ beat.
- Tap and count aloud. Then tap and say the words.
- Look at the music and not at your hands.

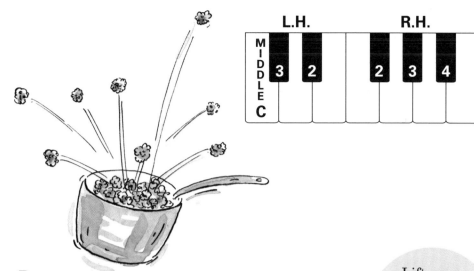

 CD 21, 22, 23 • MIDI 8

Popping Popcorn

Lift your hands off the keys, wrists *first*, and place them in your lap.

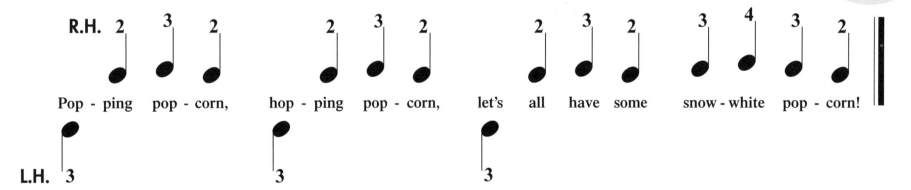

R.H. 2   3   2   2   3   2   2   3   2   3   4   3   2

Pop - ping pop - corn,   hop - ping pop - corn,   let's all have some   snow - white pop - corn!

L.H. 3   3   3

Time to Compose:

- Using the 2 or 3 black-key groups, make up a piece about squirrels. Some ideas: squirrels laughing and chattering, leaping, sleeping

★ **Practice your piece as many times as it takes to remember it completely!**

FJH2223

15

The Half Note ♩

This is a **half note**. It gets 2 beats.

How to do it:

Clap once for each ♩ note, and then hold your hands together for 1 more beat.

Count: 1 - 2   1 - 2
"clap hold, clap hold"

♩ = ♪ ♪

Tapping Feet

Clap and count aloud:

1	*1*	*1*	*1*	*1*	*1*	*1 – 2*
Dance	a -	bout	with	tap -	ping	feet.

1	*1*	*1*	*1*	*1*	*1*	*1 – 2*
Step	in	time	to	feel	the	beat!

Now point to each note and say the words!

Practice steps:

- Circle the two half notes.
- Tap the rhythm with your "Perfect Piano Hands."

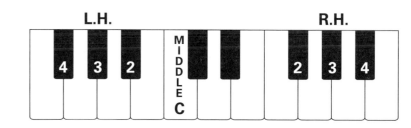

 CD 24, 25, 26 • MIDI 9

Kitten in the Tree

These are repeated notes.

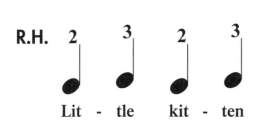

R.H.   2   3   2   3   4   4   4

Lit - tle   kit - ten   in   the   tree,

Please come down and   play with me!

L.H.   2   3   2   3   4   4   4

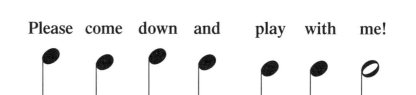

- Did you notice your 4 little hills on each hand?
- Where else did you play repeated notes?

DUET PART: (student plays 1 octave higher)

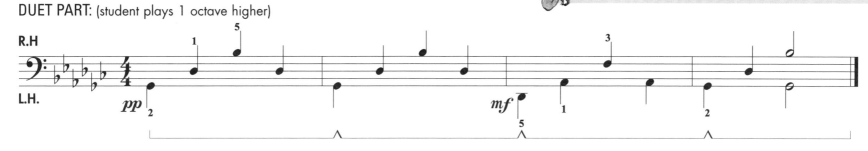

R.H

L.H.

pp   mf

- Write the counting below. The first 3 words have been done for you.

- Tap and count, then tap and say the words.
  (Remember your R.H. and L.H.!)

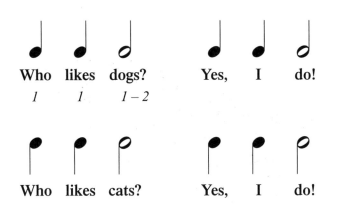

Who   likes   dogs?   Yes,   I   do!
1   *1*   *1 – 2*

Who   likes   cats?   Yes,   I   do!

- Draw 4 half notes for the R.H.
  Write in the counts.

1 - 2

- Draw 4 half notes for the L.H.
  Write in the counts.

1 - 2

Time to Compose:

- Using ♩ and ♩ notes, make up a piece about a boy in a boat or a girl with an umbrella.
  Play the piece high, low, and in the middle of the piano.

Melody

A **melody** is a string of notes that make a tune. Melody is what we sing or hum!

Do you have a favorite melody?

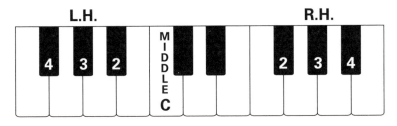

Melodies

R.H. 4 3 4 3 4 3 2

I   like play - ing   mel - o - dies,   glid - ing   on   the   black   keys.

L.H. 3 2 3 2 3 4

- Check for strong fingers (no dents!)
- Relax your wrists

repeat sign
(Play the piece again.)

DUET PART: (student plays 1 octave higher)

R.H.

L.H. *mf*

The Musical Alphabet

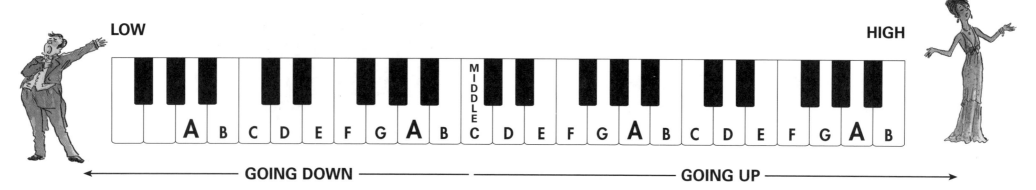

The white keys have letter names.

The first 7 letters of the alphabet are:

A B C D E F G

See how they repeat on the keyboard.

- Starting with A, write the letter name on the keys below.
- Then say the letter name of the keys while you play them.

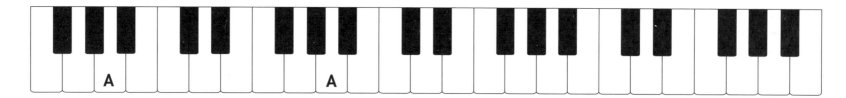

FJH2223

C D E

Practice steps:

- Play a group of 2 black keys. Then find the 3 white keys in front of the 2 black keys.
- On the keyboard below, circle all the groups of 2 black keys and then write in all of the C D E's.

CD 30, 31, 32 • MIDI 11

Graceful Bird

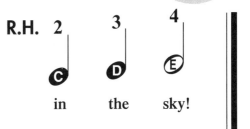

R.H. 2   3   4

C   **D**   Ⓔ

in   the   sky!

Lift your hands off, wrist first.

soar - ing high

C   **D**   Ⓔ

L.H. 4   3   2
cross over

Notice that each group of notes moves up.

R.H. 2   3   4

C   **D**   Ⓔ

go - ing   by,

Grace - ful   bird

C   **D**   Ⓔ

L.H. 4   3   2

Time to Compose:

- Make up a piece using C D E.
- Will it go higher or lower?

- Was *Graceful Bird* steady?
- Did you play with "Perfect Piano Hands?"

DYNAMIC SIGNS tell you how loud or soft to play.

forte (*f*) means to play loudly.

piano (*p*) means to play softly.

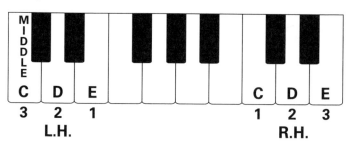

Practice steps:

- Circle the *f* and *p* signs.
- Plan the sounds.
- Show your teacher where repeated notes are.

Eating Ice Cream!

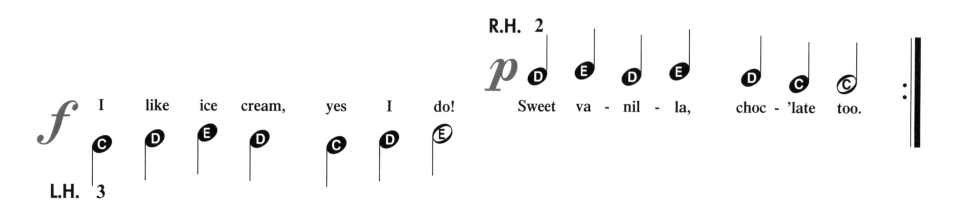

I like ice cream, yes I do! Sweet va - nil - la, choc - 'late too.

- On the repeat say the letter name of each note.
- Did you hear *f* and *p*?

DUET PART: (student plays as written)

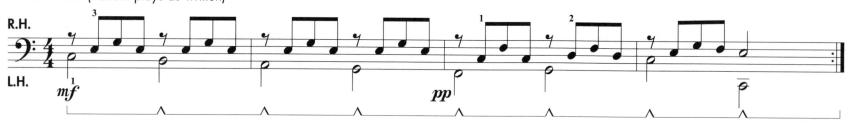

22

FJH2223

Bar Lines

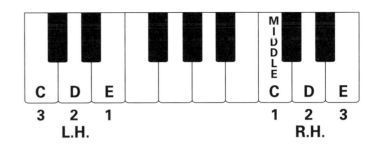

Bar lines look like this: | | Do you see them in this piece? The space between the bar lines is called a MEASURE. Placing bar lines in the music helps to group the beats so the same number of beats are in each measure.

 CD 36, 37, 38 • MIDI 13

The Orchestra

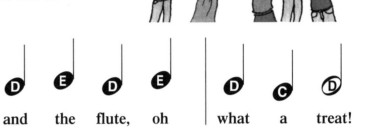

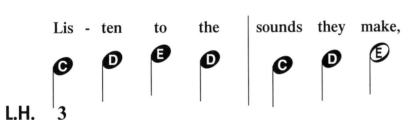

R.H. 1

C D E D | C D E | D E D E | D C D

Hear the trum - pets, | tap your feet; | and the flute, oh | what a treat!

f *p*

C D E D | C D E | D E D E | D C C

Lis - ten to the | sounds they make, | then they'll stop and | take a break!

L.H. 3

f *p*

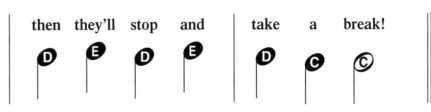

• Did you feel your 4 little hills on each hand? 〰〰

DUET PART: (student plays 1 octave higher)

mf 5 1 5 5 *pp* 2 3 *mf* 4 1 5 5 *pp* 1 2 5

F G A B

Practice steps:

- Play a group of 3 black keys. Then find the 4 white keys in front of the 3 black keys.
- On the keyboard below, circle all the groups of 3 black keys and then write in all of the F G A B's.
- Add in the bar lines.

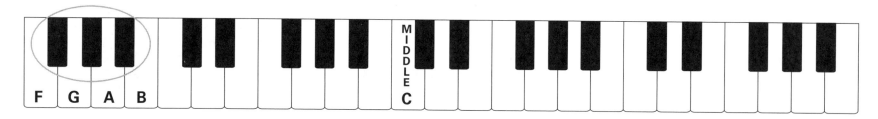

The F G A B Song

CD 39, 40, 41 • MIDI 14

R.H. 1

F G A B

F   G   A   B.

sim - ply known as

F G A B

L.H. 4
cross over

R.H. 1   2   3   4

F G A B

four new keys, they're

f   I   am learn - ing

F G A B

      4   3   2   1

L.H. 4

- Was the rhythm steady?
- Did you feel and see a natural "C" shape between fingers 1 and 2?

24

FJH2223

Practice steps:

- How many measures are in the piece? _____
- Tap and count aloud.
- Tap and say the finger numbers.
- Tap and say the letter names.
- Point to each note and say the words.

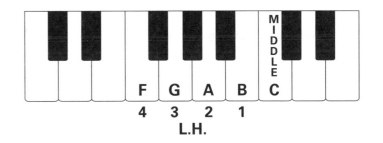

The Wishing Well

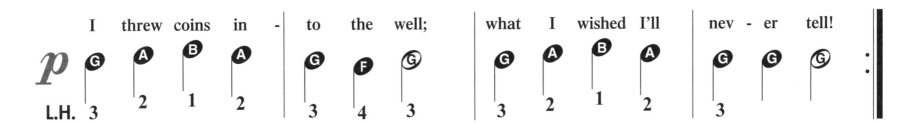

Time to Compose:

- Make up a piece using FGAB and ♩ and ♩ notes.
- Use your R.H.
- What will you wish for?

DUET PART: (student plays as written)

Finding the White Keys

1. Finish writing the musical alphabet below.

A B C D E F G

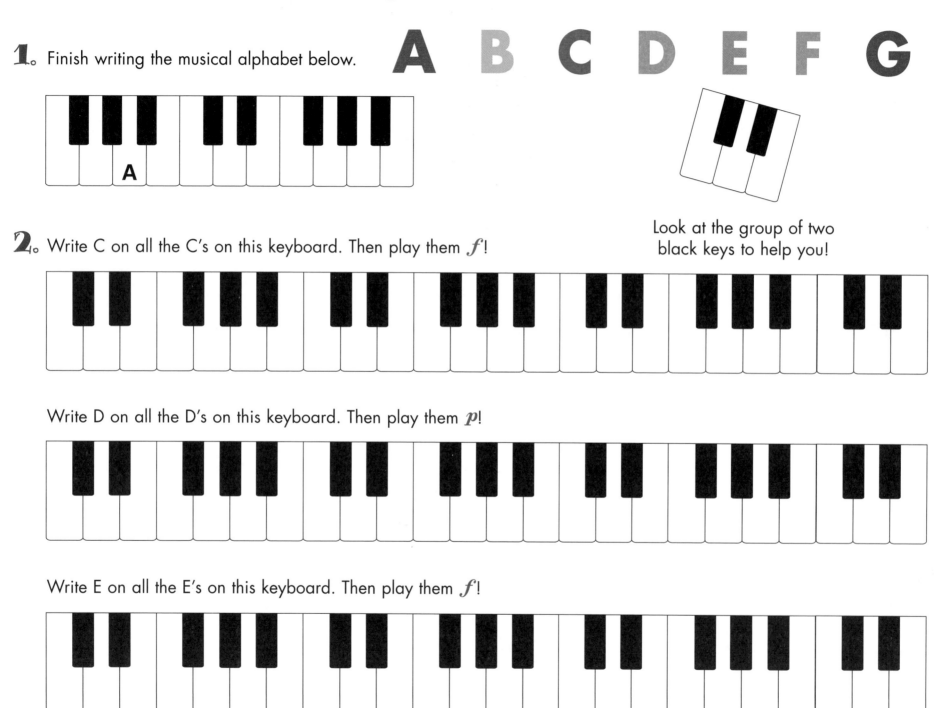

Look at the group of two black keys to help you!

2. Write C on all the C's on this keyboard. Then play them *f*!

Write D on all the D's on this keyboard. Then play them *p*!

Write E on all the E's on this keyboard. Then play them *f*!

FJH2223

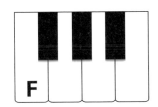

F is to the left of a group of 3 black keys.

Write **F** on all the F's on the keyboard. Then play them p!

B is to the right of a group of 3 black keys.

Write **B** on all the B's on the keyboard. Then play them f!

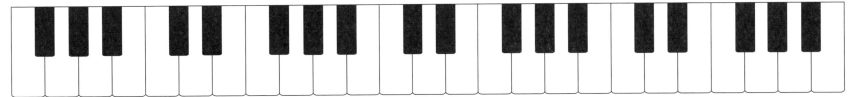

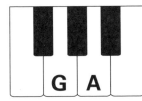

G and **A** are in the middle of a group of 3 black keys.

Write **G** and **A** on all the G's and A's on the keyboard. Then play them p!

The Whole Note ○

```
C   D   E               MIDDLE C   D   E
3   2   1                      1   2   3
    L.H.                           R.H.
```

○ This is a **whole note**. It gets 4 beats.

How to do it:

Clap once for each ○, and then hold for 3 more beats.

Count:
○
1 - 2 - 3 - 4
"clap hold, hold, hold,

○
1 - 2 - 3 - 4
clap hold, hold, hold"

CD 45, 46, 47 • MIDI 16

Check!
Natural
"C" shape!

Mary Had a Little Lamb

R.H. 3

𝆑

E D C D | E E E | D D D | E E E |

Mar - y had a lit - tle lamb,
Ev - 'ry - where that Mar - y went,

lit - tle lamb,
Mar - y went,

lit - tle lamb,
Mar - y went,

DUET PART: (student plays 1 octave higher)

R.H.
5
3

L.H. *mf* 1

FJH2223

It's Matching Time!

Draw a line from the left to the correct answer on the right.

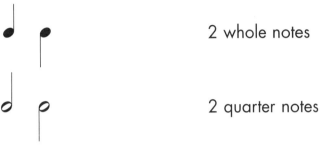

2 whole notes

2 quarter notes

2 half notes

Lift your hands off the keys, wrists *first*, and place them in your lap.

| Mar - y | had | a | lit - tle | lamb, | its | fleece | was | white | as | snow. |
| Ev - 'ry - where | that | | Mar - y | went, | the | lamb | was | sure | to | go. |

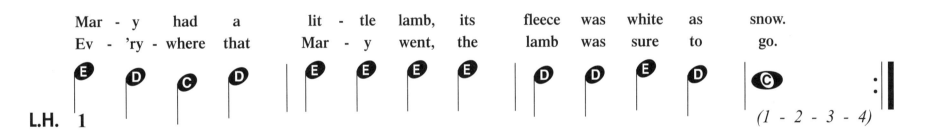

L.H. 1

(1 - 2 - 3 - 4)

- Did you play this piece with energy?
- Was it steady?
- Did you play with "Perfect Piano Hands?"

The **time signature** at the beginning of a piece tells you the number of beats in each measure.

$\frac{4}{4}$ The upper 4 means there are 4 beats in every measure.

$\frac{4}{4}$ The bottom 4 means a ♩ gets one beat.

Chugging Trains

Practice steps:

- Add the missing bar lines.
- Circle the whole notes.
- Finish writing the counting under the notes.
- Then clap and count aloud.

Chug - ging   up   and   chug - ging   down   and   all   a - round   the   rail - road   track;

You write: 1   1   1   1

Blow   the   horn!   Down   the   tracks!

Time to Compose:

- Make up a piece using any white keys.
  Use the rhythm and words of "Chugging Trains."

- Listen to your teacher play a pattern. Circle the one you hear.

1. ♩♩ ♩ or ♩ ♩♩   2. o | ♩♩♩ | or ♩♩♩ | o |

FJH2223

Middle C Position

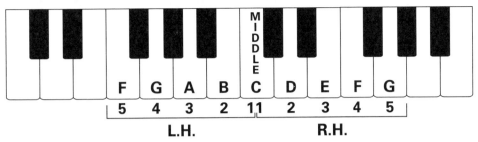

Practice steps:

- Add the time signature.
- Find and circle the repeated notes.
- Keep your eyes on the music and not on your hands.

Yellow Spaceship

• Check for your 8 hills.

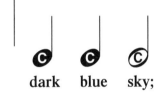

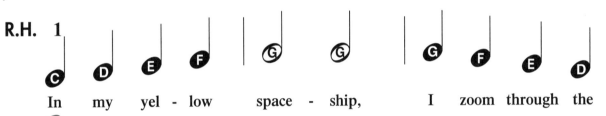

R.H. 1

C D E F G G G F E D C C C

In   my   yel - low   space - ship,   I   zoom through the   dark   blue   sky;

f

Here   I   watch   the   plan - ets   and   com - ets   that   go   rush - ing   by.

C B A G F F F F G A B C C C

L.H. 1

p

Move up to the next "C" on the repeat.

DUET PART: (student plays 1 octave higher)

Steps

A **step** is the distance from 1 white key to the next white key.

step up

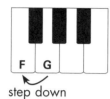
step down

A step is also called a **2nd**.

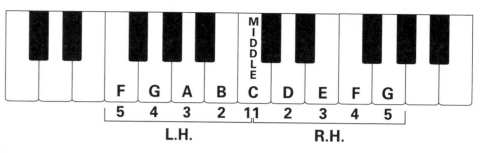

F	G	A	B	MIDDLE C	D	E	F	G
5	4	3	2	1 1	2	3	4	5

L.H.   R.H.

Check!
Natural
"C" shape!

CD 51, 52, 53 • MIDI 18

The Ice Cream Truck

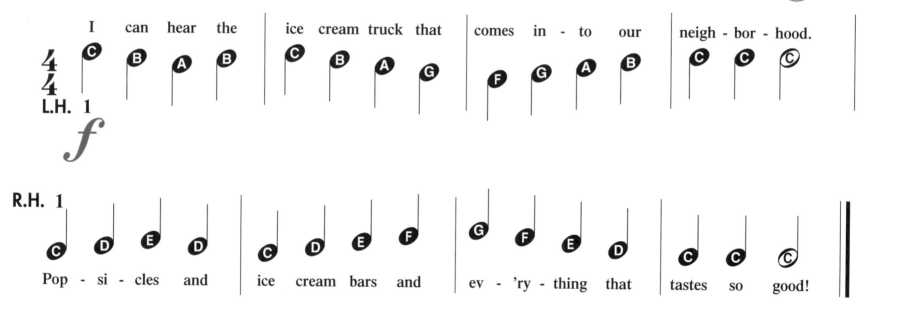

I can hear the ice cream truck that comes in-to our neigh-bor-hood.

Pop-si-cles and ice cream bars and ev-'ry-thing that tastes so good!

DUET PART: (student plays 1 octave higher)

- Is this piece cheerful or sad?
- Did you hear the steps?

32

FJH2223

 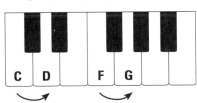 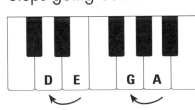 

Steps going up:

Steps going down:

1. Write the letter name of the key a step UP from each marked key.

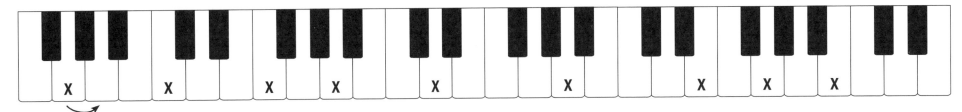

2. Write the letter name of the key a step DOWN from each marked key.

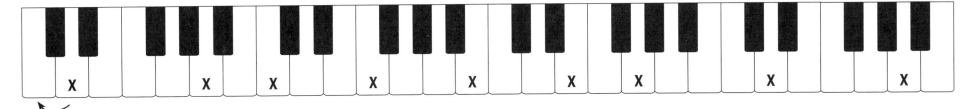

3. Write the correct letter names below. Then play them on the piano.

C _D_   E ____   F ____   B ____   G ____   A ____
step up   step up   step down   step down   step up   step down

• Your teacher will play steps going up and going down. Tell your teacher which one you hear.

The Grand Staff

Mozart

1. This is a STAFF. It has 5 lines and 4 spaces.

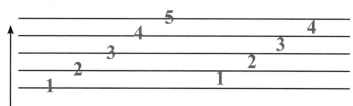

The lines and spaces are numbered from the bottom to the top.

2. This is the GRAND STAFF.

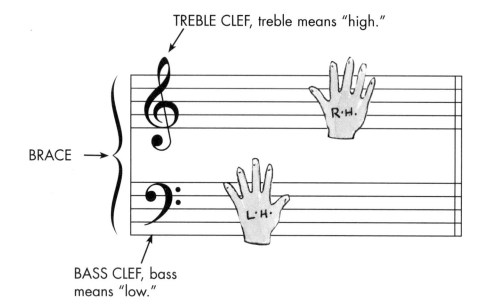

TREBLE CLEF, treble means "high."

BRACE →

BASS CLEF, bass means "low."

3. Middle C is a very important note. It is called a **Guide Note**. Draw 2 Middle C's.

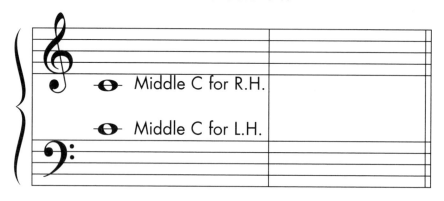

Middle C for R.H.

Middle C for L.H.

4. Write "L" for line note and "S" for space note. Name which space or line the note is.

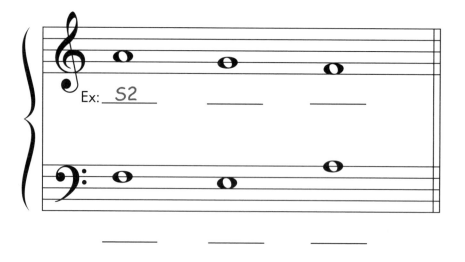

Ex: ___S2___ _____ _____

_____ _____ _____

FJH2223

Middle C is on a little piece of line between the 2 staffs.

Middle C for R.H.	1st line below - R.H.
Middle C for L.H.	1st line above - L.H.

Middle C Position

The Middle C High Step

CD 54, 55, 56 • MIDI 19

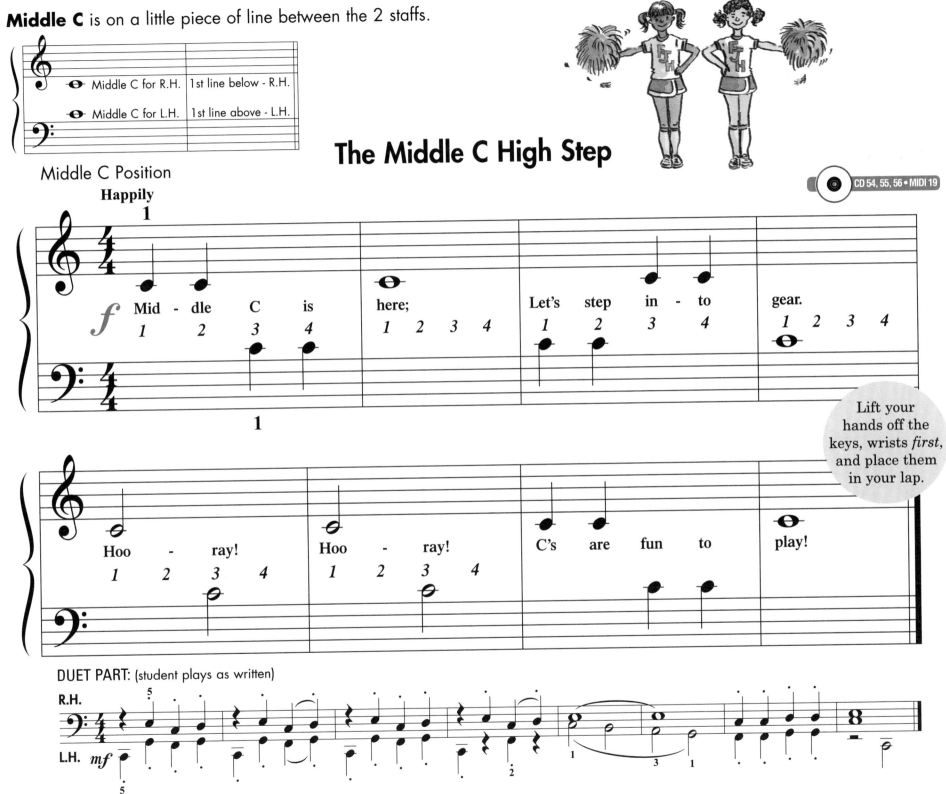

Happily

f Mid - dle C is here; Let's step in - to gear.
1 2 3 4 1 2 3 4 1 2 3 4 1 2 3 4

Hoo - ray! Hoo - ray! C's are fun to play!
1 2 3 4 1 2 3 4

Lift your hands off the keys, wrists first, and place them in your lap.

DUET PART: (student plays as written)

R.H.
L.H. *mf*

FJH2223

Middle C and Treble G

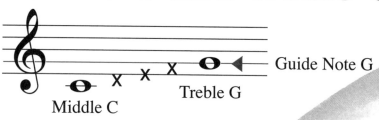

Middle C — Guide Note G — Treble G

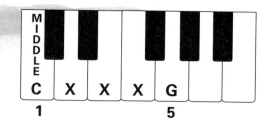

The **Treble Clef** has another name — **G Clef**, because it shows where Treble G is on the staff.

CD 57, 58, 59 • MIDI 20

A Rainbow

Brightly

f Look - ing out my win - dow, I can see a rain - bow,

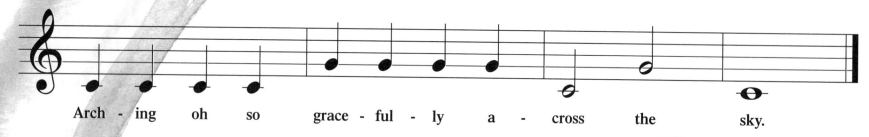

Arch - ing oh so grace - ful - ly a - cross the sky.

- Did you play brightly?
- Can you sing this song?

DUET PART: (student plays 1 octave higher)

FJH2223

Middle C and Bass F

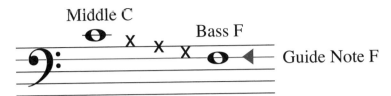
Middle C · Bass F · Guide Note F

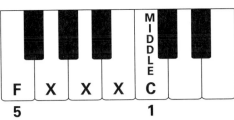

The **Bass Clef** has another name—**F Clef**, because it shows where Bass F is on the staff.

CD 60, 61, 62 • MIDI 21

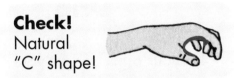
Check! Natural "C" shape!

Moonlight

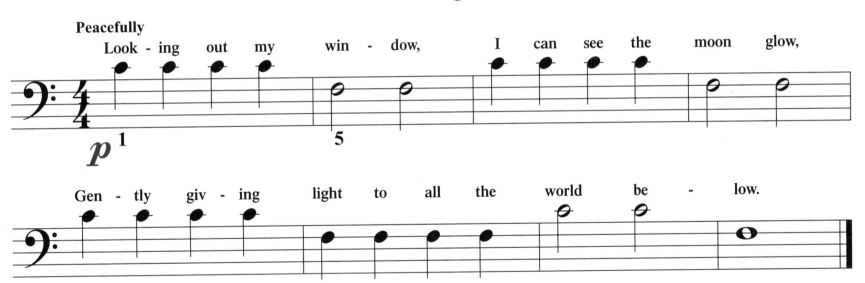

Peacefully

Look - ing out my win - dow, I can see the moon glow,

p

Gen - tly giv - ing light to all the world be - low.

DUET PART: (student plays 1 octave higher)

R.H.

L.H. *pp* with pedal

"Drip-Drop-Roll"

Drip

- Lift your arms and let your fingers hang down. Pretend water can **drip** through your fingertips to your thighs.

Drop

- Let your arms **drop** to your thighs. Can you feel the weight of your arms drop? This is arm weight.

Roll

- **Roll** your wrists forward onto your fingertips, and lift your wrists and forearms.

Note to Teachers: Using finger 3, have students play any key of their choice. When they drop their arm using a little weight, they make a quiet sound. Using more arm weight, they get a louder sound. Have them experiment with the sound and the technique.
Remind students to notice the natural "C" shape between fingers 1 and 2.

FJH2223

Guide Notes

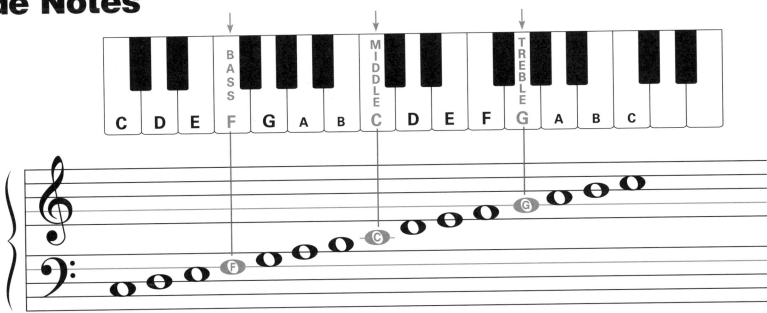

 CD 63, 64, 65 • MIDI 22

Guide Notes

Use the **"Drip-Drop-Roll"** technique you know.

Slowly

p

C C
Guide notes

G G G G
are im - por - tant!

C C
Mem - o -

F F F F
rize these guide notes!

• Play on the outside tip of your thumbnail.
• Notice your 8 knuckles. They look like 8 small hills.

Practice steps:

- Block (play together) Guide Notes Middle C and Treble G with your R.H.

- Then, block Guide Notes Middle C and Bass F with your L.H.

- Look at the music and not at your hands.

Use the **"Drip-Drop-Roll"** technique you know.

Middle C Position

City Sounds

Hear those loud | cit - y sounds; | BEEP! BEEP! | all a - round.

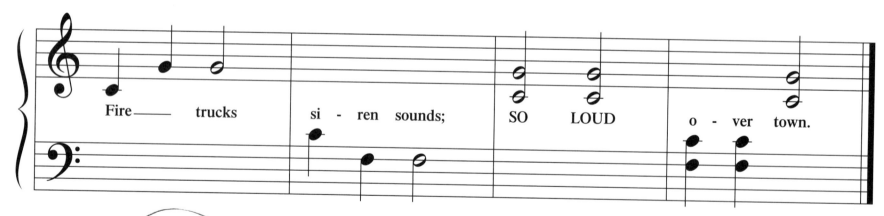

Fire—— trucks | si - ren sounds; | SO LOUD | o - ver town.

Time to Compose:

- Make up a piece using guide notes.
  Add the pedal to hear the different sounds!

- Did the piece sound lively?

FJH2223

1. Write the name of the Guide Notes below each note. The first one is done for you.

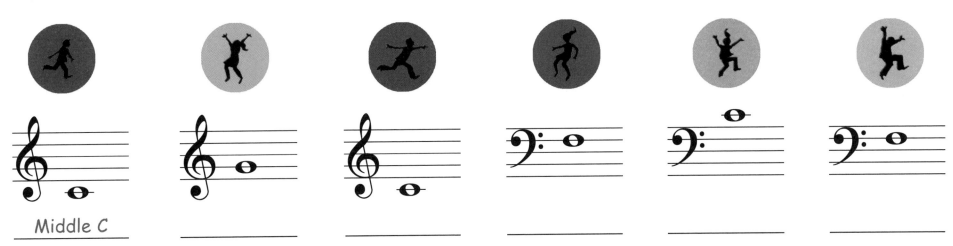

Middle C

2.

Parrots love to repeat what they hear!

- Your teacher will play one example from each set.
- Can you play it back? (Look at the patterns below and listen carefully!)
- Circle the one you hear.

1. ♩ ♩ or ♩ ♩   2. ♩ ♩ ♩ or ♩ ♩ ♩

For teacher use:

3.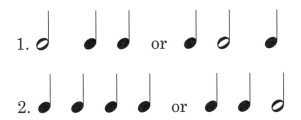

- Your teacher will tap one example from each set.
- Tap the pattern you hear. Then circle it.

1. 𝅗𝅥 ♩ ♩ or ♩ 𝅗𝅥 ♩

2. ♩ ♩ ♩ ♩ or ♩ ♩ 𝅗𝅥

Practice steps:

- Which two Guide Notes will you play? _____ and _____
- Point to the measures where your hands play together.
- Which finger plays Treble G? _____

Two-Note March

CD 69, 70, 71 • MIDI 24

Lively

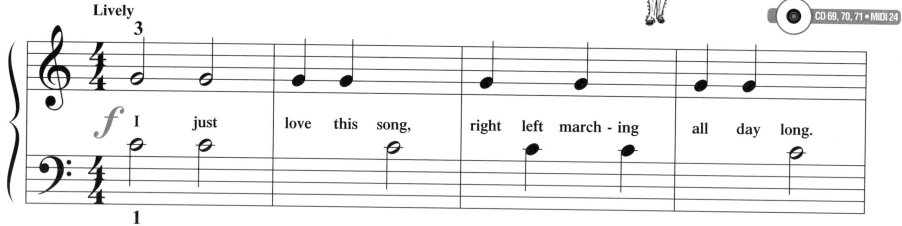

I just love this song, right left march - ing all day long.

When the mu - sic nears the end, I just want to play a - gain!

DUET PART: (student plays 1 octave higher)

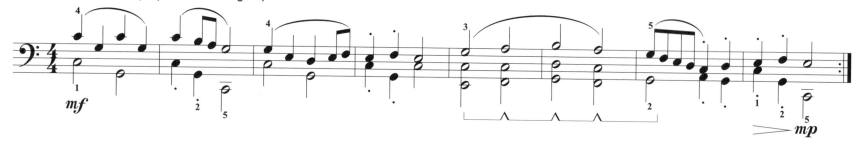

FJH2223

Time Signature Review

- Fill in the missing bar lines.
- Then clap and count aloud.

1.

2.

- Place the correct finger number(s) on each line.
- Then tap the rhythm pattern with the correct finger(s).

1.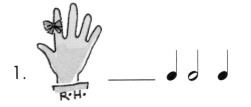

2.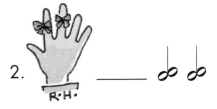

3.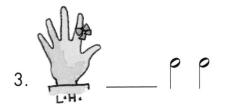

4.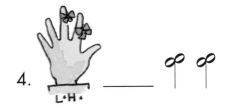

- Your teacher will play some steps.
- Are the notes played together (blocked) or one after the other (broken)?
- Write "BL" for blocked, and "BR" for broken.

1. _____   2. _____

3. _____   4. _____

Steps in the Bass Staff

1. Remember to use your L.H. when you see this clef:

A step on the staff is from a line to a space,
or a space to a line:

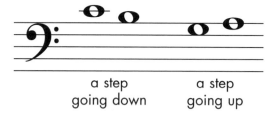

a step
going down

a step
going up

2. Now find A—B—C.

L.H.

3. Mozart's practice steps:

- Point to each note and count aloud.
- Then point and say the words.
- Play and count aloud.
- Play and sing the words.

Mozart

CD 72, 73, 74 • MIDI 25

Bass Clef Melody

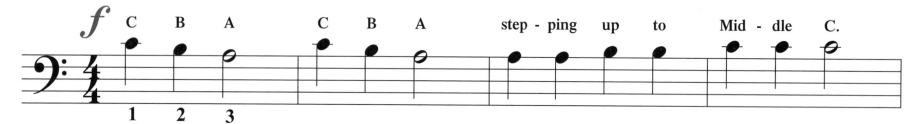

f   C   B   A   C   B   A   step - ping   up   to   Mid - dle   C.

1   2   3

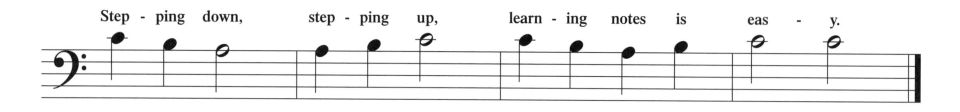

Step - ping   down,   step - ping   up,   learn - ing   notes   is   eas - y.

FJH2223

Steps in the Treble Staff

1. Remember to use your R.H. when you see this clef:

- Play this step:
  Is it going up
  or down? _____

  line to space

- Play this step:
  Is it going up
  or down? _____

  space to line

2. Now find C—D—E.

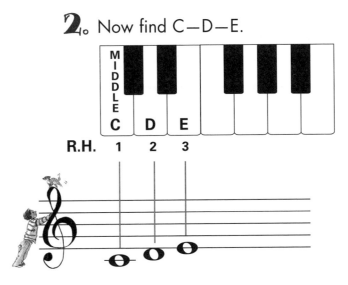

R.H. 1 2 3

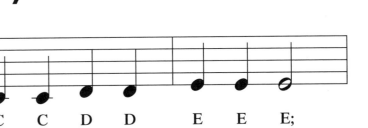

3. Use the same practice steps Mozart gave you on p. 44.

Use the same practice steps Mozart gave you on p. 44.

CD 75, 76, 77 • MIDI 26

Treble Clef Melody

Beethoven

f Step - ping up, *p* step - ping down, *f* C C D D E E E;

Step - ping down, step - ping up, E E D D C C.

- Did you count aloud?
- Did you hear a change in **dynamics** (*f* and *p*)?

The Dotted Half Note $\boxed{\quad \downarrow. = 3 \text{ beats}}$

$\downarrow.$ = 3 beats

$\downarrow. = \downarrow \, \downarrow \, \downarrow$

$\downarrow. = \downarrow \quad \downarrow$

$\downarrow. = \downarrow \, \downarrow$

$\downarrow.$ This is a **dotted half note**. It gets 3 beats.

How to do it:

Clap once for each $\downarrow.$ note, and then hold
your hands together for 2 more beats.

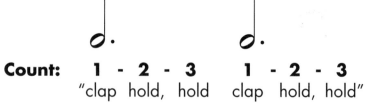

$\downarrow. \qquad\qquad \downarrow.$

Count: **1 - 2 - 3   1 - 2 - 3**
  "clap hold, hold   clap hold, hold"

- Clap the rhythm. Notice a **NEW** Time Signature.
- Then finish writing in the counts.

1   2   3

- Fill in the missing bar lines. The first one has been done for you.
- Then clap and count aloud.

Time to Compose:

- Make up a piece in $\frac{3}{4}$ time.
- With your L.H., use the rhythm on the left.
- Play only A-B-C in the melody.
- What animal will it be about?

FJH2223

Focus on B

Practice steps:

- Point to each note and count aloud.
- Then point and say the letter name of each note.
- Point to each note and say the direction of the notes, like "step up," "step down," or "repeat."

B is a step below MIDDLE C.
Find the B's in your music!

A Big Snow Cone

CD 78, 79, 80 • MIDI 27

Happily

I want a really big snow cone;
I like the trop - i - cal fla - vors;

On a hot day it's re - fresh - ing and cool.
Red, green, and blue are the best, as a rule.

DUET PART: (student plays 1 octave higher)

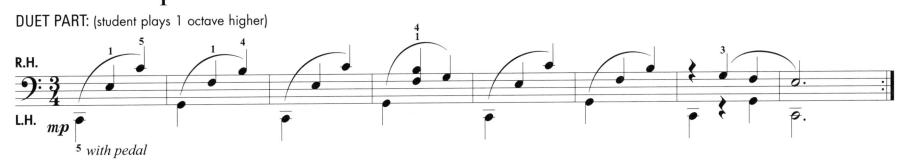

with pedal

FJH2223

Practice steps:

- Circle the 𝅗𝅥. notes.
- Tap and count aloud.

 CD 81, 82, 83 • MIDI 28

Poor Dog Named "Bright"

Moving along

f Poor dog named "Bright" ran off with all his might; Be -

Lift your
hands off the
keys, wrists *first*,
and place them
in your lap.

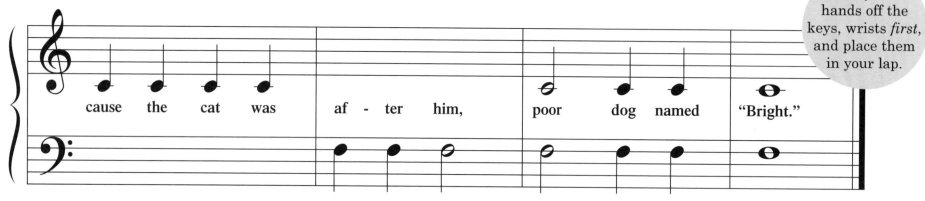

cause the cat was af - ter him, poor dog named "Bright."

DUET PART: (student plays 1 octave higher)

R.H.

L.H.

mf

FJH2223

Steps D E F

step up
(space to line)

step up
(line to space)

steps going up

• Track the notes with a line to show the steps and repeated notes.

CD 84, 85, 86 • MIDI 29

Ringing the Bells

This note is _____.

Brightly

f Ring - ing the bells as they shim - mer so bright,

p soft win - ter snow fall - ing all through the night.

Sing the note names on the repeat.

• Did you hold the 𝅗𝅥. for 3 beats?

DUET PART: (student plays as written)

mf   *pp*

FJH2223

49

Music Dictionary

Music term	Definition	Found on page:
arm weight	how the arms should feel at the piano	38
bar lines	lines in the music that organize the rhythm	23
bass clef	notes for the left hand use this clef. It is also called the 'F' clef.	34
clef	a sign that shows the position of notes on a staff	34
dotted half note	gets three beats	46
double bar line	shows the piece has ended	12
dynamics	how loudly or softly to play, *forte* or *piano*	22
forte (*f*)	an Italian word that means to play "loudly" or "strongly"	22
half note	gets two beats	16
measure	a group of beats, separated by bar lines	23
melody	a string of notes that make a tune you can sing along with or hum	19

FJH2223

Steps (2nds):

space to line   line to space

Certificate of Achievement

_____

Student

has completed the

THE ALL-IN-ONE APPROACH

to Helen Marlais'
Succeeding at the Piano®

PREPARATORY A

You are now ready for

PREPARATORY B

THE
F·J·H
MUSIC
COMPANY
INC.

Frank J. Hackinson

_____   _____

Date   Teacher's Signature